Informing the legislative debate since 1914

The United Arab Emirates (UAE): Issues for U.S. Policy

Kenneth Katzman

Specialist in Middle Eastern Affairs

September 25, 2014

Congressional Research Service

7-5700

www.crs.gov

RS21852

Summary

The UAE has been a significant U.S. partner in Gulf security for more than two decades, and the alliance is extending to the U.S.-led effort against the Islamic State organization. A 1994 U.S.-UAE defense cooperation agreement (DCA) provides for U.S. military use of several UAE facilities, and about 5,000 U.S. military personnel are in the UAE at those facilities. The UAE was the first Gulf state to order the most sophisticated missile defense system sold by the United States, demonstrating support for U.S. efforts to assemble a regional missile defense network against Iran. The UAE has helped pressure Iran by implementing financial and economic sanctions against it, while avoiding antagonizing that large neighbor by maintaining trade and commercial ties with it. The UAE has sought to use a relaxation of tensions produced by ongoing nuclear negotiations between Iran and the international community to try to resolve a territorial dispute with Iran. Yet, suggesting continued wariness of Iranian ambitions in the Gulf, the UAE has sought U.S. assurances that the United States will maintain its commitment to Gulf security.

Regionally, the UAE has become increasingly assertive against extremist Islamic organizations, even to the point of undertaking some military action in post-Qadhafi Libya without consulting the United States. The UAE has financially backed moderate Islamist rebels forces in Syria who are fighting not only the Asad regime but also the Islamic State that holds territory there and in Syria. This stance has led the UAE to join the U.S.-led anti-Islamic State coalition, including engaging in airstrikes in Syria against it as of September 2014. In concert primarily with de-facto leader of the Gulf Cooperation Council (GCC) Saudi Arabia, the UAE is giving financial assistance to the military-led government of Egypt that in July 2013 ousted the elected president Mohammad Morsi, a Muslim Brotherhood leader. The UAE and Saudi Arabia also have worked to undermine other Muslim Brotherhood-related organizations in the region, including Hamas. These activities have put the two GCC states at odds with fellow GCC state Qatar and with Turkey, which support such organizations. In 2011, the UAE joined the Saudi-led GCC intervention in another GCC state, Bahrain, to help it suppress a major uprising by its Shiite majority. Also that year, UAE pilots flew combat missions against Muammar Qadhafi of Libya and the UAE joined the GCC diplomatic effort that brokered a political solution to the unrest in Yemen. The UAE has deployed over 200 troops to Afghanistan since 2003.

Regarding UAE domestic politics and human rights issues, the UAE's relatively open borders and economy have won praise from advocates of expanded freedoms in the Middle East, but have also produced social ills such as abuses of foreign workers and human trafficking. The social and economic freedoms have not translated into significant political change; the UAE remains under the control of a small circle of leaders who allow citizen participation primarily through traditional methods of consensus-building. To date, these consultation mechanisms, economic wealth, and reverence for established leaders have enabled the UAE to avoid wide-scale popular unrest. Since 2006, the government has provided some formal popular participation in governance through a public selection process for half the membership of its quasi-legislative body, the Federal National Council (FNC). But, the leadership has resisted any dramatic or rapid further opening of the political process and has suppressed both Muslim Brotherhood-linked Islamists and secular opposition activists.

Very few policy changes are anticipated should UAE President Shaykh Khalifa bin Zayid Al Nuhayyan leave the scene unexpectedly. He suffered a stroke on January 24, 2014, leaving his younger brother Shaykh Mohammad bin Zayid, who already had substantial governing responsibilities, in charge. The extent of President Khalifa's current governing role is unclear.

Contents

Figures

Tables

Contacts

Governance, Human Rights, and Reform[1]

The United Arab Emirates (UAE) is a federation of seven emirates (principalities): Abu Dhabi, the oil-rich capital of the federation; Dubai, its free-trading commercial hub; and the five smaller and less wealthy emirates of Sharjah, Ajman, Fujayrah, Umm al-Qaywayn, and Ras al-Khaymah. Sharjah and Ras al-Khaymah have a common ruling family—leaders of the Al Qawasim tribe. After Britain announced in 1968 that it would no longer ensure security in the Gulf, six "Trucial States" decided to form the UAE federation in December 1971; Ras al-Khaymah joined in 1972. The UAE federation has completed a major leadership transition since the death of its key founder, Shaykh Zayid bin Sultan Al Nuhayyan, long-time ruler of Abu Dhabi and UAE president, on November 2, 2004.

Shaykh Zayid's first son, Shaykh Khalifa bin Zayid al-Nuhayyan, born in 1948, was elevated from Crown Prince to ruler of Abu Dhabi upon Zayid's death. In keeping with tradition, although not formal law, Khalifa was subsequently selected as UAE president by the leaders of all seven emirates who comprise the "Federal Supreme Council." The ruler of Dubai traditionally serves concurrently as Vice President and Prime Minister of the UAE; that position has been held by Shaykh Mohammad bin Rashid Al Maktum, architect of Dubai's modernization drive, since the death of his elder brother Shaykh Maktum bin Rashid Al Maktum in January 2006. Shaykh Mohammad bin Rashid also continued as federation Defense Minister. At its review of senior leadership posts on November 3, 2009, the Federal Supreme Council decided that Shaykh Khalifa and Shaykh Mohammad bin Rashid would serve another five-year term. The review was mostly a formality because UAE leadership posts almost always change only in the event of death of an incumbent. The Federal Supreme Council meets four times per year to establish general policy guidelines, although the leaders of the seven emirates consult frequently with each other.

The leadership of the UAE was put into some doubt by Shaykh Khalifa's stroke on January 24, 2014. He underwent surgery and senior family members say his health has recovered,[2] but he has not been appearing in public. Some press reports indicate that Shaykh Khalifa has been discussing succession scenarios with other senior Nuhayyan figures, suggesting his health might be worse than is being portrayed publicly. His overall governing function is being performed by his heir apparent, his younger brother and the third son of Shaykh Zayid, Crown Prince Shaykh Mohammad bin Zayid al-Nuhayyan, born in 1961. Shaykh Mohammad had already been assuming significant day-to-day governing responsibilities over the past few years. Several senior UAE officials are other brothers that are close to Shaykh Mohammad, including Foreign Minister Abdullah bin Zayid, deputy Prime Minister Mansur bin Zayid, Interior Minister Sayf bin Zayid, and UAE national security adviser Hazza bin Zayid.

---

[1] Much of this section is from the State Department's country report on human rights practices for 2013 (released February 27, 2014), *http://www.state.gov/documents/organization/220592.pdf. International Religious Freedom Report* for 2013 (July 28, 2014), http://www.state.gov/j/drl/rls/irf/religiousfreedom/index htm?year=2013&dlid=222317#wrapper;and the *Trafficking in Persons Report for 2014* (July 24, 2014), http://www.state.gov/documents/organization/226849.pdf. See also the Human Rights Watch "World Report 2014." https://www hrw.org/world-report/2014/country-chapters/united-arab-emirates

[2] http://gulfbusiness.com/2014/07/abu-dhabi-crown-prince-says-uae-president-healthy-dismisses-rumours/#.U9e-NSg1Png

The Crown Prince of Dubai is Shaykh Mohammad bin Rashid's son, Hamdan bin Mohammad Al Maktum, who heads the "Dubai Executive Committee," the equivalent of a cabinet for Dubai emirate. Under a Dubai-level reorganization announced in January 2010, five committees were set up to advise the Executive Committee on major issues.

Table 1. Some Basic Facts About the UAE

Population	5.47 million, of whom about 1 million (about 18%) are citizens.
Religions	The citizenry is almost all Muslim, of which 85% are Sunni and 15% are Shiite. Of the total population, 76% is Muslim; 9% is Christian; and 15% is other—but primiarily Buddhist or Hindu.
Ethnic Groups	11% Emirati (citizenry); 29% other Arab and Iranian; 50% South Asian; 10% Western and other Asian expatriate
Size of Armed Forces	About 50,000
Inflation Rate (2013)	About 1.1%
GDP Growth Rate for 2013	4% estimated by IMF
GDP (purchasing power parity, ppp, 2012)	$270 billion. Per capita is $30,000 ppp
Oil Exports	About 2.7 million barrels per day
Foreign Exchange and Gold Reserves	About $67 billion, but some estimates of the value of its sovereign wealth fund investments run into the several hundreds of billions of dollars.
U.S. Exports to the UAE (2013)	$24.5 billion, making UAE the largest U.S. export market in the Arab world and a 50% increase since 2011. Goods sold to UAE are mostly machinery, commercial aircraft, industrial materials, and other high value items.
Imports from UAE by the United States (2013)	$2.3 billion. None of that amount was crude oil.
U.S. citizens resident in UAE	About 60,000
Major Projects	Dubai inaugurated "Burj Khalifa," world's tallest building, on January 4, 2010. Burj al-Arab hotel in Dubai bills itself as "world's only 7-star hotel." Abu Dhabi has built local branches of Guggenheim and Louvre museums.

Sources: CIA, *The World Factbook*; U.S. Census Bureau, Foreign Trade Statistics.

The leaders of the other individual emirates are Dr. Sultan bin Muhammad Al Qassimi (Sharjah); Saud bin Saqr Al Qassimi (Ras al-Khaymah, see below); Humaid bin Rashid Al Nuaimi (Ajman); Hamad bin Muhammad Al Sharqi (Fujayrah); and Saud bin Rashid Al-Mu'alla (Umm al-Qaywayn). Shaykh Saud of Umm al-Qaywayn, who is about 64 years old, was named leader of that emirate in January 2009 upon the death of his father, Shaykh Rashid Al-Mu'alla. These five emirates, often called the "northern emirates," tend to be more politically and religiously conservative and homogenous than are Abu Dhabi and Dubai, which are urban amalgams populated by many Arab, South Asian, and European expatriates.

In Ras al-Khaymah, there was a brief leadership struggle upon the October 27, 2010, death of the ailing longtime ruler, Shaykh Saqr bin Mohammad Al Qassim. He was succeeded by Shaykh Saud bin Saqr, who had been crown prince/heir apparent since 2003, when the ruler removed

Saud's elder brother, Shaykh Khalid bin Saqr, from that position. During 2003-2010, using public relations campaigns in the United States and elsewhere, Shaykh Khalid claimed to remain as heir apparent even though the UAE federal government had repeatedly stated that his removal from that position was legitimate and that he held no official position in the UAE. Shaykh Khalid's home in Ras al-Khaymah was surrounded by security forces the night Shaykh Saqr died, enforcing the succession of Shaykh Saud.

Figure 1. Map of United Arab Emirates

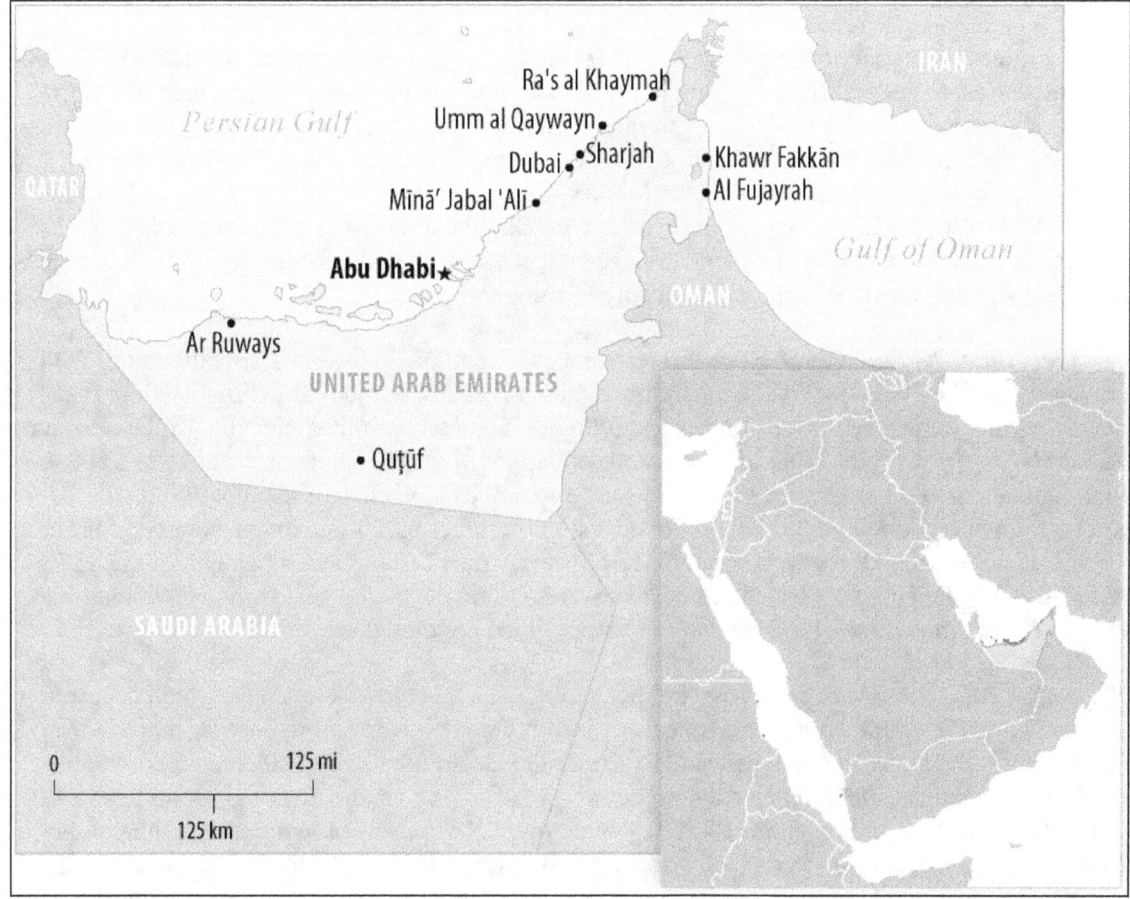

Source: CRS Graphics.

Political Reform and Responses to Opposition

The UAE is not considered by any U.S. or outside organization to be a democracy, but its perceived social tolerance and distribution of ample wealth have rendered the bulk of the population apparently satisfied with the political system. With the exception the youth and intellectual-led activism in the UAE inspired by the Arab uprisings of 2011, and discussed below, there has been little clamor for more rapid political reform. The government has moved against underground activism using arrests, prosecutions, and monitoring of the Internet and social media.

A Top-Driven Modest Reform Process

UAE leaders long argued that Western-style democracy, including elections for the country's leadership, is not needed in UAE because Emiratis are able to express their concerns directly to the leadership through traditional consultative mechanisms. Most prominent among these channels are the open *majlis* (councils) held by many UAE leaders. UAE leaders maintain that Western-style political parties and elections for a legislature or other representative body would inevitably aggravate long dormant schisms among tribes and clans and potentially cause Islamist factions to become radical.

The UAE leadership had long provided a minor measure of popular representation through an all-appointed 40-seat Federal National Council (FNCThe FNC can review, but not enact or veto, federal legislation, and the government frequently accepts the FNC's legislative recommendations. The FNC can question, but not impeach, ministers. It has conducted such "grillings," mostly on economic and social issues. Its sessions are open to the public. The seat distribution of the FNC is weighted in favor of Abu Dhabi and Dubai, which each hold eight seats, while Sharjah and Ras al-Khaymah have six each, and the others each have four. Each emirate also has its own all-appointed consultative council.

Elections First Held in 2006. Leadership resistance to elections to the FNC prevailed until 2006, at which time the UAE leadership apparently decided it had fallen too far behind its Gulf neighbors on political reform. In December 2006, it conducted a limited electoral process for half of the FNC seats, with the other 20 FNC seats still appointive. The 2006 electorate was to be limited to about 100 persons for each FNC seat, appointed or elected, or about 4,000 total electors. The Election Commission approved a slightly larger 6,595-person electorate, or about 160 persons per seat. Of the total electors, 1,162 were women (less than 20%). Out of the 452 candidates for the 20 FNC elected seats, there were 65 female candidates. Only one woman was elected (from Abu Dhabi), but another seven were given appointed seats.

September 24, 2011, FNC Election. In the September 24, 2011, FNC election—which occurred in the context of the "Arab spring" uprisings that inspired demands for more popular input in the Arab states—the government expanded the size of the electorate to 129,000 electors, or "voters" (30 times as many as the 2006 election process). A total of 468 candidates filed to run for the 20 seats up for election on September 24, 2011, including 85 women—little more than the number of candidates who filed to run in the 2006 process. However, the 2011 electorate was nearly half female, in contrast to the fewer than 20% electors in the 2006 process. Candidate spending was not allowed to exceed $545,000.

There was widespread press reporting of citizen apathy about the election, with little information about the election or campaigns in the media and little active campaigning. Turnout averaged about 25%, which UAE officials called disappointing, and which was apparently pulled down by the 21% turnout in the largest emirate, Abu Dhabi.

Of the 20 winners, only one was female (Sheika Isa Ghanem)—from Umm Al Quwain, one of the more conservative emirates. It was believed that female candidates would have the best chance of winning in Dubai, considered the most liberal of the emirates. Other winners were elected along tribal lines; in Abu Dhabi, three of the four who were elected are from the Al Amiri tribe. Of the 20 appointed seats, 6 appointees were women, bringing the total number of women in the FNC to 7. The government selected as FNC Speaker an appointed male member, well-known writer

Mohammad al-Murr, and Amal al-Qubaisi, one of the appointed women, as deputy speaker. She became the first woman to hold so high a position in any GCC legislative body.

However, insisting on implementing political opening at a gradual pace, the government has not implemented calls—such as a March 2011 petition signed by 160 UAE intellectuals—to transform the FNC into an all-elected body with full legislative powers.[3] Nor is the leadership allowing formal political parties. Minister of State for FNC Affairs Anwar Gargash wrote in a UAE paper (*The National*) on August 26, 2012, that "The UAE's end goal is not a liberal multiparty system. This model does not correspond with our cultural or historical development."[4] His comments came following an August 1, 2012, announcement by several Islamists of the formation of a political party called "Al Umma"—an alleged violation of UAE laws that do not grant citizen rights to form political parties.

Government Handling of Opposition

Since the 2011 Arab uprisings and dissatisfied with the slow pace of reform, some UAE intellectuals, businessmen, students, and other groups have been agitating—primarily through written editorials and Internet postings—for more political space. Some UAE youth, on social networking outlets such as Facebook and Twitter, called for a protest on March 25, 2011. It did not produce a significant demonstration, in part because the UAE government blocked some social media sites but perhaps because the demonstration did not attract broad support.

The government has attempted to address the activism and other popular demands. In March 2011, the government invested about $1.5 billion in utilities infrastructure of the poorer, northern emirates; it raised military pensions by 70%; and it introduced subsidies for some foodstuffs. In March 2013, the government announced a minor cabinet reshuffle—advertised as a "new look" to bring in youthful figures and ideas. The dynamic Suhail al-Mazroui was appointed Energy Minister, and Abu Dhabi royal family member, Shaykh Abdullah bin Mubarak al-Nuhayyan, was appointed Minister of Culture, Youth and Social Development with a mandate to reach out to UAE youth. The government's most prominent female minister, Minister of Foreign Trade Shaykha Lubna Al Qassimi, was given an even higher profile role as head of a new Ministry of Development and International Cooperation, in charge of all UAE foreign aid and cooperation with international bodies.

The government also has employed some repressive measures. Authorities generally disperse protests and public gatherings that are critical of the government or its policies. On April 8, 2011, a prominent Dubai blogger and activist, Ahmad Mansour Al Shehi, was arrested, and four other online activists were arrested later that month on charges of "publicly humiliating senior officials." All five—the so-called "UAE-5"—appeared in court on June 15 and October 2, 2011, but human rights organizations said their trials violated basic rights of the accused. The five were given jail terms in November 2011, but President Khalifa commuted their sentences and they were released.

During April and May 2011, the government dissolved the elected board of directors of the Jurist Association and the Teachers Association, two leading civil society groups, after members of their boards signed petitions for political reforms. The boards were reconstituted with government

---

[3] Al Jazeera News Network, March 9, 2011.

[4] Anwar Gargash. "Amid Challenges, UAE Policies Engage Gradual Reforms." *The National*, August 26, 2012.

appointees. The Jurists' Association's Human Rights Committee and the Emirates Human Rights Association (EHRA) are the only two recognized local human rights organizations in the country.

The government has continued to seek ways to suppress criticism spread via social media. The main recent tool the government has used is a "cybercrimes decree" issued by President Khalifa on November 13, 2012 (Federal Legal Decree No. 5/2012). It established a legal base to prosecute and jail people who use information technology to agitate against the regime or demand more political rights. According to Human Rights Watch, Article 28 of the decree provides for imprisonment and large fines for anyone who uses information technology to incite actions that endanger state security or infringe on the public order. Article 30 provides for life imprisonment for anyone using such technology to advocate the overthrow or change of the system of governance. On December 23, 2013, a UAE court sentenced a U.S. national, Shezanne Cassim, to one year in jail for violating the decree by making a video parodying youths in Dubai. An Emirati citizen, Obaid al-Zaabi, was arrested under the decree in December 2013 for "offending the Supreme Court" for his sending of Twitter messages ("tweets") criticizing the lack of free speech in the UAE. He was acquitted on June 23, 2014, but purportedly remains detained.[5]

Efforts Against Islamists/Muslim Brotherhood

The UAE leadership asserts that political Islamist movements linked to the Muslim Brotherhood—particularly a UAE affiliate of the Brotherhood called Islah (Reform)—constitute a threat to the state. Islah is one of the oldest and best organized groups in the UAE, first appearing in UAE in 1974, and has its base of support in the poorer and more religiously conservative northern emirates. Islah does not have a history of committing violent acts in UAE or elsewhere. The UAE government began to move against these movements more assertively after Muslim Brotherhood member Mohammad Morsi came to power in Egypt in 2012. UAE officials have accused Islah of obtaining financial and other support from the Muslim Brotherhood in Egypt, reflecting an apparent UAE fear that Brotherhood-linked Islamist groups in UAE could join with secular activists to mount a major challenge to the government, as happened in Egypt in 2011. The UAE has also accused Islah of having ties to Yusuf Qaradawi, a pro-Brotherhood Egyptian cleric resident in neighboring Gulf state Qatar,[6] and it has asked Qatar to expel Qaradawi. The split between Qatar and the UAE and other GCC states over the Muslim Brotherhood and other political Islamist movements has often precluded unified GCC action on several regional issues, as discussed later in this report.

The UAE crackdown on the Brotherhood inside the UAE began in December 2011, when it revoked the citizenship of a Muslim Brotherhood figure who headed an institution called the "Innovative Thinking Center" in Dubai emirate. On April 20, 2012, an Islah member who belongs to the royal family of Ras al-Khaymah, Dr. Sultan al-Qasimi, was arrested. Another, arrested on July 16, 2012, was human rights lawyer Mohammad al-Roken, who provided legal services to Islah and also to the "UAE-5" mentioned above. On November 12, 2012, a UAE court rejected an appeal by seven Islamists against the Interior Ministry's revocation of their citizenship.

On March 4, 2013, a trial began for 94 UAE nationals arrested from 2011 to 2013 and accused of forming a secret Muslim Brotherhood-affiliated network allegedly plotting to overthrow the UAE government. Human rights groups say some of the suspects were tortured and deprived of proper

---

[5] Matt Duffy. "UAE Twitter Activist Not Guilty but Still in Custody." Al Monitor, July 24, 2014.

[6] "UAE Targets Muslim Brotherhood in Crackdown on Dissent," BBC, September 26, 2012.

legal representation. On July 2, 2013, the UAE State Security Court sentenced 69 of the 94 to prison terms of between 7 and 15 years for "plotting to overthrow the state." The other 26 were acquitted. While that trial was underway, on June 19, 2013, UAE authorities referred another 30 persons, of which 20 are Egyptian nationals, to that court for alleged connections to the Muslim Brotherhood in Egypt. Their trial started on November 5, 2013, and they were convicted in January 2014. On January 21, 2014, the Federal Supreme Court ordered the closure of all offices and branches of the Muslim Brotherhood.

U.S. Democracy Promotion Efforts and UAE Restrictions

The United States has long sought to promote democracy, rule of law, and civil society in the Persian Gulf region, including in UAE, with relatively small programs and quiet diplomacy. This policy has been implemented through State Department programs to promote student and women's political participation, entrepreneurship, legal reform, civil society, independent media, and international trade law compliance—funded largely by State Department programs such as the Middle East Partnership Initiative (MEPI). These programs are conducted with the acquiescence of the UAE government. The U.S. Embassy in Abu Dhabi houses a MEPI office/staff that runs the MEPI programs throughout the Gulf region.

Still, suggesting its sensitivity to activities that could empower domestic opposition groups, the UAE has acted against some U.S.-funded democracy promotion groups. On April 5, 2012, the government closed the National Democratic Institute (NDI) office in Dubai, and briefly barred both its American director and Serbian deputy director from leaving the country. NDI had been working for four years, with license from the UAE government and U.S. funding, to promote women's rights and to advise on municipal governance. The government also shut down the office of the German democracy-promotion organization, the Konrad Adenauer Foundation, which was performing similar work. UAE government representatives continue to insist that NDI and the Adenauer Foundation were meddling in its internal affairs and that such activity was unacceptable. U.S. public criticism of these UAE government actions has been relatively minor and episodic. In 2013 and thus far in 2014, official accounts of virtually all high-level U.S.-UAE meetings have focused almost entirely on regional and security issues.

Similarly, international criticism of the UAE crackdown on perceived oppositionists has been muted. On October 26, 2012, the European parliament adopted a resolution criticizing the crackdown. The UAE government claimed the resolution was based on erroneous information from UAE bloggers and other activists. Several European governments with close financial or security ties to the UAE, including Italy and France, made statements indicating disagreement with the European parliament resolution. And, the resolution did not prevent the UAE from assuming a seat on the U.N. Human Rights Council on November 12, 2012.

General Human Rights-Related Issues

The State Department human rights report for 2013, released February 27, 2014, analyzes the government's actions against dissent, discussed above. In addition, as do past State Department reports, the report for 2013 asserts that there are unverified reports of torture, government restrictions of freedoms of speech and assembly, and lack of judicial independence.[7] Earlier, a

---

[7] http://www.state.gov/documents/organization/220592.pdf

Human Rights Watch "World Report 2014," issued in January 2014, issued similar findings on the issue of free expression as well as other human rights issues discussed below. Some domestic civil society organizations monitor the human rights situation in the UAE, including the Emirates Center for Human Rights (ECHR).

Press and Research Institute Freedoms

Prior to its efforts to ferret out unrest, the UAE had drawn praise for its free-wheeling media. The post of Information Minister was abolished in 2006 to allow for full media independence. A "National Media Council" directly oversees all media content, and provisions governing media licensing do not clearly articulate the standards the government will apply in evaluating license applications. Restrictions do not apply to the "Free Zones" in UAE in which major foreign media organizations operate. In April 2009, a revised media law was adopted that allowed for penalties against journalists who personally criticize UAE leaders.

Since 2010, there have been increasing restrictions on research institutes, several of which had opened in UAE in the 1990s because of the perceived free expression. The government applied increasingly strict criteria to renewing the licenses of such research institutes and some, such as the Dubai-based Gulf Research Center (GRC), left the UAE entirely. In November 2012, the UAE ordered the Rand Corporation to close its office in Abu Dhabi, which was focused on research in education, public safety, and environmental health. UAE officials also have denied entry to some academics and human rights organizations officials, such as those from Human Rights Watch, who have been critical of the UAE human rights record.[8] In February 2013, the American University of Sharjah cancelled a conference on the "Arab Spring" because a speaker from the London School of Economics was denied entry.

Justice/Rule of Law

The UAE has a dual court system. Sharia (Islamic law) courts adjudicate criminal and family law matters. Civil courts, based on French and Egyptian legal systems, adjudicate civil law matters. The federal judiciary in the UAE began in 1973 with the establishment of the Federal Supreme Court. The federal judiciary now comprises the Federal Supreme Court, Federal First Instance Courts, and Federal Appeal Courts. The Federal Supreme Court consists of a president and a maximum number of five judges appointed by a decree issued by the President of the UAE and confirmed by the Federal Supreme Council. The Federal Supreme Court looks into matters such as various disputes erupting between the member emirates or between one or more emirate and the UAE federal government, the constitutionality of federal and other laws and legislations, conflicts of jurisdiction between the federal and local judicial authorities in the country, conflict of jurisdiction between the judicial authority in one Emirate and another, and crimes directly affecting the interests of the UAE federation. It also interprets the provisions of the constitution and questioning ministers and senior federal officials for official misconduct. Under the constitution, each emirate has the right to join the federal judiciary system or maintain its own judicial system, and Abu Dhabi, Dubai, and Ras al-Khaymah have opted for the latter arrangement. According to the State Department, foreign nationals hold many positions in the judiciary, making them subject to political influence because they can be deported easily.

---

[8] CRS conversations with UAE officials. 2012-2014.

Furthermore, local rulers review criminal and civil cases before referral to prosecutors, and these political leaders review sentences as well—and the rulers' decisions supersede those of any court.

A 2012 amendment to the UAE consittution set up a "Federal Judicial Council" chaired by UAE President Khalifa. His deputy on that body is the chair of the Federal Supreme Court. UAE officials said the additional judicial body was needed to decide on all matters relating to the judiciary, judges, and judicial policies and legislation. Human rights groups objected to the fact that the body is chaired by the UAE President, but the UAE government stressed that the same constitutional amendment enshrined judicial independence.

Many observers note that justice in UAE is selective. For example, on January 10, 2010, a UAE court acquitted the UAE president's brother, Shaykh Issa bin Zayid Al Nuhayyan, on charges of torturing an Afghan merchant. He was acquitted even though there was a video available of Shaykh Issa driving over his legs with a sport vehicle. The UAE court ruled that Shaykh Issa was not liable because he was taking prescription drugs that affected his actions.

The UAE justice system has often come under criticism when expatriates are involved. Even though the UAE promotes itself as a popular tourist destination, Western expatriates have sometimes been arrested for sexual activity on UAE beaches. Arrests of noncitizens increased during the 2008-2009 financial crisis, possibly out of citizen frustration that globalization and dramatic economic expansion have led to bursting of the economic "bubble" in UAE. In 2007, human rights groups criticized the conservative-dominated justice system for threatening to prosecute a 15-year-old French expatriate for homosexuality, a crime in UAE, when he was raped by two UAE men; the UAE men were later sentenced for sexual assault and kidnapping. In August 2012, a 78-year-old pediatrician from South Africa, Cyril Karabus, was imprisoned for alleged issues of malpractice related to his six-week service as a doctor in Abu Dhabi in 2002.[9] He was jailed for two months and prevented from leaving the UAE until June 2013. In July 2013, a Norwegian woman was sentenced to 16 months in jail by a Dubai court for having sex outside marriage after she reported being raped. She was released in late July 2013 after the case caused an outcry from human rights organizations.

Women's Rights

Progress on women's political rights has been steady—as exemplified by the November 2011 appointment of a woman as deputy FNC Speaker. Observers say the UAE is perhaps the only country in the Middle East where women are fully accepted working in high-paying professions such as finance and banking. There are four women in the cabinet: Shayha Lubna al-Qassimi (discussed above); Mariam al-Roumi, minister of social affairs; and two ministers without portfolio—Reem al-Hashimi and Maitha al-Shamsi. Seven women are in the Federal National Council, as discussed above, and six women serve on the 40-seat consultative council in Sharjah emirate. About 10% of the UAE diplomatic corps is now female; none served prior to 2001. In September 2013, the UAE appointed a female, Lana Nusseibeh, as UAE Permanent Representative to the United Nations. In November 2008, Dubai emirate appointed 10 female public prosecutors. The UAE Air Force has four female fighter pilots, one of whom has been qualified to fly the UAE's U.S.-made F-16 combat aircraft. The percentage of female voters in the September 2011 FNC election process was nearly 50%, as discussed above.

---

[9] Lydia Polgreen. "Emirates' Laws Trap a Doctor Just Passing Through." *New York Times*, April 12, 2013.

More broadly, women in the UAE are still at a legal disadvantage relative to men, for example in divorce cases and other family law issues. As of December 2011, UAE women are allowed to pass on their citizenship to their children—the first GCC state to allow this. Many domestic service jobs are performed by migrant women, and they are denied basic legal protections such as limits to work hours.

Religious Freedom

The State Department report on international religious freedom for 2013, issued July 28, 2014, generally repeated previous year's assessments.[10] The constitution provides for freedom of religion but also declares Islam as the official religion of the country. The death penalty for conversion from Islam remains on the books but is not known to be enforced. In practice, non-Muslims in UAE are free to practice their religion; there are 35 Christian churches built on land donated by the ruling families of the various emirates, but there are no Jewish synagogues or Buddhist temples. There is a Sikh temple that shares a building with one of two existing Hindu temples. Buddhists, Hindus, Sikhs, and Jews conduct religious ceremonies in private homes and in hotels or other rented locations without interference.

The Shiite Muslim minority is free to worship and maintain its own mosques, but Shiite mosques receive no government funds and there are no Shiites in top federal posts. At times, the government has acted against non-UAE Shiite Muslims because of their perceived support for Iran, Syrian President Bashar Al Assad, Lebanese Hezbollah, and the mostly Shiite opposition in Bahrain. In 2012, the government closed a Shiite madrassa (school) and, in May 2012, it denied permission to UAE Shiites to host a meeting of worldwide Shiites. In March 2013, the government deported 30 Shiite Muslims, including those from Pakistan, Iraq, Syria, and Lebanon. The UAE and other GCC states have taken some steps to expel Lebanese Shiites to pressure Lebanese Hezbollah for its direct military support of the Assad regime in Syria.

Labor Rights

The law prohibits all forms of compulsory labor, but it is not enforced effectively. On several occasions, foreign laborers working on the large, ambitious construction projects in Dubai have conducted strikes to protest poor working conditions and nonpayment of wages. There have been numerous and persistent allegations that foreign workers are housed in cramped "labor camp" conditions, have their passports held, are denied wages or paid late, are forced to work long hours, are deported for lodging complaints, and are subjected to many other abuses. In May 2014, the government arrested foreign laborers striking to protest many of the conditions discussed above in the course of building a facility for New York University's (NYU's) branch in Abu Dhabi.[11] NYU apologized to the workers for the alleged poor conditions and said the university would work with Abu Dhabi authorities to investigate and rectify the working conditions. In the past, the Labor Ministry has addressed similar complaints by penalizing employers and establishing a process (June 2008) to have workers' salaries deposited directly in banks.

---

[10] http://www.state.gov/j/drl/rls/irf/religiousfreedom/index htm?year=2013&dlid=222317#wrapper

[11] Ariel Kaminer and Sean O'Driscoll. "Workers at N.Y.U.'s Abu Dhabi Site Faced Harsh Condtions." *New York Times*, May 19, 2014.

Human Trafficking

Other social problems might be a result of the relatively open economy of the UAE, particularly in Dubai. The UAE is still considered a "destination country" for women trafficked from Asia and the former Soviet Union. The Trafficking in Persons report for 2014, released in July 2014, again placed the UAE in "Tier 2"—the same level as in the reports for the four prior years. The Tier 2 placement for 2014 was determined, as it was in the prior years, on the grounds that the UAE does not meet the minimum standards for eliminating human trafficking, but is taking significant efforts to do so.

The 2014 report notes, as do previous years' reports, that UAE authorities have prosecuted and punished sex trafficking offenders. However, the UAE efforts against forced labor—including unlawful withholding of passports, restrictions on movement, nonpayment of wages, and physical or sexual abuse of workers—have been less significant. An issue in previous years had been trafficking of young boys as camel jockeys, but that issue was largely alleviated with repatriation of many of those trafficked, and the use of robot jockeys at camel races. In October 2013, the UAE government set up a fund to help human trafficking victims rebuild their lives; the funds will be channeled through the Ewa'a organization, in conjunction with the UAE's "National Committee to Combat Human Trafficking." Ewa'a runs shelters in several UAE emirates for trafficking victims. The government opened its first shelter for male sexual trafficking victims in late 2013.

Foreign Policy and Defense

Following the 1990 Iraqi invasion of Kuwait, the UAE determined that it needed a closer security relationship with the United States. The UAE did not necessarily perceive a direct threat from Saddam Hussein's Iraq, which is at the north end of the Persian Gulf, but the UAE apparently saw the United States as the key actor in containing Iranian power. The cooperation has taken on numerous dimensions, including UAE purchase of advanced missile defense capabilities designed to counter Iranian ballistic missiles, U.S. military deployments in UAE intended to demonstrate resolve to Iran, and UAE participation in U.S.-led air operations in regional crises. Beyond the Gulf, the UAE has been increasingly assertive since the 2011 Middle East uprisings to try to preserve regional stability.

UAE cooperation with the United States complements UAE participation in all GCC security and foreign policy coordination mechanisms. The GCC leaders have emphasized improving coordination among them as Iran and the international community have negotiated an agreement to limit Iran's nuclear program. Most, if not all, the GCC leaders appear to believe that a final deal could cause the United States to de-emphasize its commitments to Gulf security. The GCC summit in Kuwait during December 10-11, 2013, agreed to a plan, subject to further study, for more intra-GCC cooperation such as a joint military command. The summit also resulted in a decision to establish a GCC maritime security coordination center, part of which is to be a new "Gulf Academy for Strategic and Security Studies" to be located in Abu Dhabi. U.S. officials, including Defense Secretary Chuck Hagel on visits to the region in 2013 and 2014, have sought to reassure the Gulf states of an enduring U.S. commitment to Gulf security, no matter the outcome of nuclear talks with Iran.

One obstacle to greater GCC defense cooperation is a schism among some of the GCC states over rival approaches to regional political Islamist movements such as the Muslim Brotherhood, as discussed further below. The UAE's past border disputes and other disagreements with Saudi Arabia occasionally flare. A 1974 "Treaty of Jeddah" with Saudi Arabia formalized Saudi access to the Persian Gulf via a corridor running through UAE, in return for UAE gaining formal control of villages in the Buraymi oasis area. And, the UAE and some of the other smaller Gulf states are wary of ceding too much GCC authority to Saudi Arabia. All of the GCC states apparently prefer to deal with the United States bilaterally rather than as a GCC bloc.

Security Cooperation with the United States/Defense Cooperation Agreement (DCA)

The framework for U.S.-UAE defense cooperation is a July 25, 1994, bilateral Defense Cooperation Agreement (DCA), the text of which is classified.[12] The DCA initially was accompanied by a separate "Status of Forces Agreement" (SOFA) giving U.S. military personnel in UAE certain legal immunities, but several incidents caused the UAE to void the SOFA and legal incidents are now handled on a "case-by-case basis." Under the DCA, the UAE has allowed U.S. equipment pre-positioning and U.S. warship visits at its large Jebel Ali port, which is capable of handling aircraft carriers, and it permitted the upgrading of airfields in the UAE that were used for U.S. combat support flights during Operation Iraqi Freedom (OIF) and continued to be used for flights in support of U.S. operations in Afghanistan.[13]

The United States and UAE have also established a "Joint Strategic Military Dialogue" to better integrate U.S. capabilities with those of the UAE. The Dialogue is to include UAE development of a defense plan that will facilitate joint U.S.-UAE planning in case of attack on the UAE.[14] Chairman of the Joint Chiefs of Staff General Martin Dempsey headed the session of the Dialogue in late May 2014.

According to UAE and U.S. officials, there are about 5,000 U.S. forces in the UAE—up substantially from 800 before OIF. The U.S. forces in UAE are mostly Air Force personnel, deployed primarily at Al Dhafra air base and who operate KC-10 refueling aircraft and several types of surveillance aircraft such as the Global Hawk and the AWACS (Airborne Warning and Control System).[15] Some U.S. personnel reportedly are stationed at naval facilities at Fujairah. In April 2012—possibly to signal additional resolve over Iran's nuclear program—the United States reportedly deployed several "Stealth" F-22 Raptor combat aircraft to Al Dhafra.[16]

The U.S.-UAE defense pact has also reportedly included U.S. training of UAE armed forces; UAE forces are relatively small—about 51,000. To address the persistent manpower problems, the UAE cabinet has begun drafting legislation to set up a new national defense and reserve force, to include mandatory military training.

The quality of the UAE force has benefitted substantially from the U.S. training conducted under the DCA. About 350 UAE military personnel study and train in the United States each year,

---

[12] Some provisions are discussed in Sami Hajjar, *U.S. Military Presence in the Gulf: Challenges and Prospects* (U.S. Army War College: Strategic Studies Institute), March 2002, p. 27.

[13] Jaffe, Greg. "U.S. Rushes to Upgrade Base for Attack Aircraft." *Wall Street Journal*, March 14, 2003.

[14] Author conversations with UAE officials. July 2014.

[15] http://www.globalsecurity.org/military/facility/dhafra htm.

[16] *Washington Post*, April 28, 2012.

mostly through the Foreign Military Sales program, through which the UAE buys most of its U.S.-made arms. U.S. military officers say that UAE operators of HAWK surface-to-air missile batteries are on par with U.S. operators of that system and that UAE fighter pilots demonstrated their combat capability in operations in Libya in 2011. Other observers say that UAE special operations forces are highly proficient. At the Air Warfare Center near Al Dhafra Air Base, UAE and U.S. forces conduct extensive exercises on early warning, air and missile defense, and logistics. The UAE also hosts the Integrated Air and Missile Defense Center, a major training facility for Gulf and U.S.-GCC cooperation on missile defense. Since 2009, UAE Air Force personnel have participated in the yearly Desert Falcon exercises at Nellis Air Force Base in Nevada, according to UAE representatives.

The UAE has also hired private parties to train some of its forces. The UAE confirmed on May 15, 2011, that it had retained the U.S. private firm Reflex Responses, to provide "operational, planning, and training support" to the UAE military. This followed a *New York Times* report that the UAE had hired the firm, which is run by Eric Prince, who founded the Blackwater security contractor, to a $529 million contract to build a foreign mercenary battalion to help defend the UAE from internal revolt or related threats.[17] The State Department investigated the reports to determine whether the contract violated any U.S. laws controlling the export of U.S. defense technology and expertise, but no findings were announced. *Defense News* reported on November 25, 2013, that a U.S. firm, Knowledge International, has provided 125 former U.S. Army officers to help improve the organization and performance of UAE land forces.

U.S. and Other Arms Sales

The UAE views arms purchases from the United States as enhancing the U.S. commitment to UAE security, and the United States views the sales as enhancing the U.S.-led Gulf security architecture by building up indigenous GCC capabilities and promoting inter-operability. From 2007 to 2010, the UAE agreed to acquire $10.4 billion worth of U.S. defense articles and services through the Foreign Military Sales program—more than any other country in the world except Saudi Arabia.[18] Until 2008, the most significant buy was the March 2000 purchase of 80 U.S. F-16 aircraft, equipped with the Advanced Medium Range Air to Air Missile (AMRAAM) and the HARM (High Speed Anti-Radiation Missile), a deal exceeding $8 billion. Congress did not try to block the aircraft sale, although some Members questioned the AMRAAM as an introduction of the weapon into the Gulf. Earlier, in September 2006, the United States sold UAE High Mobility Artillery Rocket Systems (HIMARS) and Army Tactical Missile Systems (ATACMs), valued at about $750 million.

Among recent major sales:

- On November 4, 2010, the Defense Security Cooperation Agency (DSCA) notified Congress of two potential sales, including a $5 billion sale of AH-64 Apache helicopters (30 helicopters, remanufactured to Block III configuration).[19]

- On November 30, 2011, DSCA notified Congress of a potential sale of 4,900 Joint Direct Attack Munitions (JDAM) kits with an estimated value of $304

---

[17] http://www.nytimes.com/2011/05/15/world/middleeast/15prince.html?_r=1&partner=rss&emc=rss.

[18] CRS Report: U.S. Arms Sales: Agreement with and Deliveries to Major Clients, 2003-2010.

[19] DSCA transmittal number 10-52. http://www.dsca.mil.

million. The widespread perception was that the munitions could potentially be used to strike hard targets, such as nuclear facilities in Iran, although there are no indications the UAE would conduct such a strike on its own. The United States previously sold the UAE JDAM kits worth $326 million in January 3, 2008.

- On April 25, 2013, Secretary of Defense Chuck Hagel, visiting UAE, reportedly finalized a sale to UAE of an additional 25-30 F-16 aircraft and associated "standoff" air-to-ground munitions. The sale was in conjunction with similar weapons sales to Israel and Saudi Arabia, and which U.S. officials indicated were intended to signal resolve to Iran.[20] The agreement came about one week after President Obama met visiting Abu Dhabi Crown Prince Shaykh Mohammad at the White House on April 16, 2013. A related potential sale was notified on January 24, 2014, for equipment upgrades to these F-16s, with an estimated value of $270 million.

- On October 15, 2013, DSCA (transmittal no. 13-48) notified Congress of a potential sale of numerous precision-guided missiles for the UAE's F-16 fleet, including 20 of the advanced ATM-84 SLAM-ER Telemetry missile and 5,000 GBU-39/B "bunker buster" bombs. (The sale of the SLAM-ER represented the first sale of that weapon to a Gulf state.) The principal contractors are Boeing and Raytheon, and the estimated cost of the munitions is $4 billion.

- *Joint Strike Fighter*. Press reports say the UAE and other Gulf states are interested in purchasing the advanced F-35 "Joint Strike Fighter" if and when the United States approves it for sale to the Gulf states. UAE officials maintain that possessing the most sophisticated U.S. aircraft enhances interoperability with U.S. air forces during joint operations, such as the airstrikes against the Islamic State organization discussed below. The UAE is said to also be evaluating the French-made Rafale and the Boeing F/A-18.

- *Possible Drone Sale?* At the IDEX defense show in February 2013, the UAE reportedly agreed to a commercial sale, worth about $200 million, for Predator unmanned aerial vehicles (UAVs), although the system apparently would be unarmed and for surveillance only. Still, Defense Department officials say they have not completed formulating a policy for the sale of such equipment to the Gulf states and it is possible that the deal might not be permitted by DOD.

Coordinated Missile Defense and U.S. Efforts to Deal with the GCC as a Bloc

A key U.S. objective has been to organize an integrated Gulf-wide missile defense network against Iran's missile force, and this objective was a major factor in the formation of the "U.S.-GCC Strategic Cooperation Forum." The Forum held its first meeting on March 31, 2012, with then Secretary of State Clinton attending, in Riyadh, Saudi Arabia. Subsequently, Deputy Assistant Secretary of State Frank Rose spoke in Abu Dhabi on April 12, 2012,[21] on the missile defense issue, saying, "As our partners acquire greater missile defense capabilities, the United States will work to promote interoperability and information sharing among the GCC states. This will allow for more efficient missile defenses and could lead to greater security cooperation in the

---

[20] Thom Shanker. "Arms Deal with Israel and 2 Arab Nations Is Near." *New York Times*, April 19, 2013.

[21] U.S. Department of State Daily Digest Bulletin, April 12, 2012.

region." Then Secretary of State Clinton continued to press the issue at the second ministerial of the U.S.-GCC Strategic Cooperation Forum on September 28, 2012, held on the sidelines of the U.N. General Assembly meetings in New York. The Forum convened again on September 26, 2013, at the sidelines of the U.N. General Assembly, but focusing mainly on regional issues.

Secretary of Defense Hagel stressed the need for the integrated network in his early December 2013 trip to the region, as well as during his visit to Jeddah on May 13-14, 2014, to attend a defense ministerial meeting of the U.S.-GCC Strategic Cooperation Forum. During that visit, he also stressed the U.S. assertion that the United States seeks to work with the GCC as a bloc. A December 16, 2013, Presidential Determination to allow defense sales to the GCC as a bloc represented an effort to implement that view. The determination was intended in part to promote the Gulf-wide integrated missile defense network.[22]

The UAE is pivotal to the U.S. effort to forge a Gulf-wide missile defense network because the UAE was the first GCC to order the Terminal High Altitude Air Defense System (THAAD), the first sale ever of that sophisticated missile defense system. A sale of THAAD equipment was first announced September 9, 2008, valued at about $7 billion. However, subsequent negotiations altered the purchase somewhat; on November 2, 2012, DSCA notified Congress of a potential sale to the UAE of additional THAAD equipment: 9 launchers, 48 missiles, and associated equipment with total estimated value of $1.135 billion.[23] In September 2013, the Defense Department awarded a $3.9 billion contract to Lockheed Martin for about 300 THAAD missiles, of which about 192 would be exported to the UAE—suggesting the UAE purchase has increased since the November 2012 DSCA notification.[24] Qatar also has purchased the THAAD.

Among significant other recent missile defense sales to the UAE are the advanced Patriot anti-missile systems (PAC-3, up to $9 billion value, announced December 4, 2007). Also announced on September 9, 2008, were sales to UAE of vehicle mounted "Stinger" anti-aircraft systems ($737 million value).

Defense Relations with Other Nations and Alliances

In recent years, the UAE has sought to broaden its defense relationships. In 2004, the UAE joined NATO's "Istanbul Cooperation Initiative," which was launched that year by NATO as an effort to bolster bilateral security with Middle Eastern countries. The UAE has "observer" status in NATO and, in 2011, the UAE sent an Ambassador to NATO under a revised alliance policy approved by NATO in April 2011. In October 2013, the UAE decided to open a mission to the European Union.

The UAE is hosting other countries' forces. In January 2008 the UAE signed an agreement with then French President Nicolas Sarkozy to allow a French military presence. The facilities—collectively termed Camp De La Paix ("Peace Camp") were inaugurated during a visit by Sarkozy to UAE on May 27, 2009, and include (1) a 900-foot section of the Zayid Port for use by the French navy; (2) an installation at Dhafra Air Base to be used by France's air force; and (3) a barracks at an Abu Dhabi military camp that houses about 400 French military personnel. In

---

[22] http://www.whitehouse.gov/the-press-office/2013/12/16/presidential-determination-gulf-cooperation-council

[23] Defense Security Cooperation Agency transmittal No. 12-40. November 5, 2012.

[24] National Public Radio, September 23, 2013.

September 2014, French forces reportedly used the facility to participate in airstrikes against the Islamic State organization. UAE forces still use previously bought 380 French-made Leclerc tanks and 60 Mirage 2000 warplanes. In September 2014, the UAE also agreed to host 600 Australian forces who potentially might participate in the U.S.-led anti-Islamic State campaign.[25]

Regional and Foreign Policy Issues

The UAE and the United States have major interests in common in the region. The following sections analyze UAE policies and cooperation with the United States on these issues.

Iran

The UAE cooperates with U.S. efforts to counter Iranian power and capabilities. UAE officials have privately backed military U.S. action, if deemed necessary to set back Iran's nuclear program.[26] However, the UAE would prefer that regional tensions be resolved diplomatically, and UAE officials welcomed the November 24, 2013, interim nuclear agreement as lessening regional tensions. The UAE would also benefit economically from a reduction of sanctions on Iran and a corresponding rebound in UAE-Iran trade. Much of the trade between the two consists of reexportation of U.S. and European goods to Iran. Since 2010, when international sanctions on Iran began tightening dramatically, UAE-Iran trade has dropped from $23 billion annually to about $4 billion, a decline that has economically harmed the powerful UAE trading community. Yet, as noted, UAE officials express concern that an improvement in U.S.-Iran relations could cause the United States to reduce its commitments to the security of the Gulf.

UAE officials, particularly those from Abu Dhabi, have also long asserted that the large Iranian-origin community in Dubai emirate (estimated at 400,000 persons) could pose a "fifth column" threat to UAE stability. This large population of Iranian expatriates is a product of long-standing UAE-Iran commercial ties; many Iranian firms and individuals—primarily in the import-export business—operate from the UAE, taking advantage of the UAE's drive to position itself as a global trading and financial hub. At the same time, the UAE seeks to deny Iran any justification for aggression or adverse action against the UAE, and it allowed then Iranian President Mahmoud Ahmadinejad to hold a rally for Iranian expatriates in Dubai in May 2007. The two countries issued mutual recriminations over the UAE decision in 2008 to fingerprint Iranian visitors.

The extensive Iranian commercial presence in the UAE also gives the United States ample opportunity to enlist the UAE in a multilateral effort to stiffen international sanctions on Iran. In October 2010, the UAE government directed its banks to fully comply with the restrictions outlined in U.N. Security Council Resolution 1929 (adopted June 9, 2010). In February 2012, the Noor Islamic Bank in Dubai, which Iran used to process much of its receipts of hard currency for its oil sales internationally,[27] announced it would no longer handle transactions with Iranian banks. UAE representatives say that Iranian-owned banks that continue to operate in UAE, including Bank Saderat and Bank Melli, do so only in cash and are relatively inactive. Closing them outright would, according to UAE officials, unduly antagonize Iran.

---

[25] "Islamic State Crisis: Australia to Send 600 Troops to UAE." BBC news, September 14, 2014.

[26] Author conversations with UAE officials. 2009-2013.

[27] Alan Cowell. "Dubai Bank Reduces Ties With Iran, It Reports." *New York Times*, March 1, 2012.

The UAE and other Gulf oil producers have cooperated with U.S. efforts to reduce Iran's oil income by offering to sell more oil to countries that want to reduce their buys from Iran. Still, some small firms in the UAE continue to supply gasoline to Iran even though such activity is potentially sanctionable under the Iran Sanctions Act (P.L. 104-172, as amended). Some UAE firms have been sanctioned under the act for those sales.

Gulf Islands Dispute

Iranian actions against the UAE in the Gulf have contributed to the UAE's strategic closeness to the United States. In April 1992, Iran asserted complete control of the largely uninhabited Persian Gulf island of Abu Musa, which it and the UAE shared under a 1971 bilateral agreement. (In 1971, Iran, then ruled by the U.S.-backed Shah, seized two other islands, Greater and Lesser Tunb, from the emirate of Ras al-Khaymah, as well as part of Abu Musa from the emirate of Sharjah.) The UAE has called for peaceful resolution of the issue through direct negotiations, referral to the International Court of Justice, or through another agreed forum. The U.S. position is that it takes no position on the sovereignty of the islands, but supports the UAE's call to negotiate the dispute.

In October 2008—two months after the UAE protested Iran's opening in August 2008 of administrative and maritime security offices on Abu Musa—the UAE and Iran signed an agreement to establish a joint commission to resolve the dispute. Iran later allowed Sharjah to open power and water desalination facilities on the island. But, the dispute flared again on April 11, 2012, when then-President Ahmadinejad visited Abu Musa and spoke to the inhabitants there, mostly Iranian fishermen. The UAE withdrew its ambassador from Tehran, and UAE officials said the action undermined many months of quiet UAE-Iran diplomacy on the issue, including the naming of negotiators on both sides. Iran incurred further UAE criticism with a May 2, 2012, visit to the island by Islamic Revolutionary Guard Corps (IRGC) Commander-in-Chief Mohammad Ali Jafari to discuss making the island a tourist hub.

The November 24, 2013, interim nuclear agreement improved prospects to resolve the issue. UAE Foreign Minister Abdullah bin Zayid al-Nuhayyan visited Tehran on November 28, 2013, and obtained an agreement from Iran to begin bilateral discussions on the status of Abu Musa. Iran also reportedly began reducing its presence on the island. On December 4, 2013, Iranian Foreign Minister Mohammad Javad Zarif visited UAE and obtained an agreement in principle from President Khalifa to visit Iran in the near future. However, perhaps in part due to Shaykh Khalifa's January 2014 stroke, that visit has not taken place to date. Experts say the two countries are still discussing a possible solution under which Iran might cede control of the disputed islands in exchange for rights to the seabed around them.[28]

Iraq/Syria/The Islamic State

The UAE is emerging as a core member of the U.S.-led coalition to defeat the Islamic State organization that has taken control of significant parts of Iraq and Syria. Upon President Obama's September 10, 2014 formal announcement of the U.S. effort to build and lead a multilateral coalition to try to defeat the Islamic State in both Iraq and Syria, the UAE declared its intent to participate in the coalition. Since September 22, 2014, it has flown airstrikes against Islamic State

---

[28] Awad Mustafa. "Iran, UAE Close to Deal on Hormuz Islands." *Defense News*, December 9, 2013.

targets in Syria, although not in Iraq. Participating in the strikes was the UAE's first female combat pilot, Mariam al-Mansouri. As noted above, it is also hosting forces from other countries that are participating in the anti-Islamic State effort, including those of France and Australia. All the GCC states except Kuwait and Oman are participating in U.S.-led military operations against the Islamic State organization, although all reportedly seek to exercise caution not to cause civilian casualties that would likely be mostly among fellow Sunni Arabs. Such casualties would, according to many observers, likely provoke a backlash of domestic criticism within the GCC countries against continuing participation in the coalition.

The UAE's willingness to help defeat the Islamic State appears to be an outgrowth not only of the UAE threat perception of the Islamic State organization but also its apparent frustration at the lack of resolution of the Syria crisis that began in 2011. UAE officials maintain that the Islamic State is a major threat not only because it might try to conduct terrorist attacks but also because, in seeking to form and expand a self-declared caliphate, the organization seeks to change the way of life for most of the Arab states.

The UAE participation in the U.S.-led anti-Islamic State coalition could also reflect an intent to try to influence the objectives of the collective intervention in Syria. The UAE and the other GCC states all have long argued for U.S. action to oust Syrian President Bashar Al Assad, in part to strategically weaken Iran in the Middle East and in part to defend the Sunni Arabs who form the bulk of the Syria rebellion. The UAE and the other GCC states argue that ousting Assad and forming an inclusive new government is crucial to weaning Syrian Sunnis from supporting the Islamic State organization.

The UAE joined its GCC allies in April 2012 in offering about $100 million in funds to Syrian rebels—none of which were linked to the Islamic State—to be used for salaries and to buy weapons and services. The UAE reportedly did not supply weapons to any Syrian rebel factions.[29] As an apparent reflection of the overall schisms in the GCC, Qatar reportedly was supporting rebel factions that were rivals of those supported by the UAE and Saudi Arabia. With the GCC assistance to the rebels failing to produce tangible rebel gains, the UAE sought greater U.S. efforts to support anti-Assad rebels and compel Assad to yield to a transition regime. In June 2013 the UAE declined to host a meeting of allied defense officials on Syria, maintaining that the meeting would be unproductive without extensive U.S. participation on the Syria issue.[30]

The UAE has also sought to alleviate suffering from the Syria crisis. In March 2013, the UAE government and various UAE charity organizations (Red Crescent Authority, Khalifa bin Zayid Al Nuhayyan Foundation, and Sharjah Charity Association) donated $330 million to help Syrian refugees. The UAE separately has given $1.25 billion to Jordan to help it cope with the Syrian refugees that have fled there because of the violence. And, UAE forces have participated in the "Eager Lion" annual military exercises in Jordan intended to help insulate Jordan from any Syria conflict spillover.

UAE officials have similarly expressed frustration at deterioration of political consensus in Iraq that UAE diplomats say led to the Islamic State success there in 2014. The UAE and other GCC states have long blamed the Shiite-dominated government of Prime Minister Nuri al-Maliki of

---

[29] Author conversations with experts in Washington, D.C. 2013-2014.

[30] Mark Mazzetti, Michael Gordon, and Mark Landler. "U.S. Is Said to Plan to Send Weapons to Syrian Rebels." *New York Times*, June 14, 2013.

marginalizing the Sunni community and provoking the schism within Iraq. In June 2014, following the capture of the city of Mosul and other Sunni-inhabited cities by forces loyal to the radical Islamist group now called the Islamic State (IS), the UAE called its Ambassador to Iraq back for consultations. The UAE has praised the change of leadership in Iraq to Prime Minster Haydar Al Abbadi, but UAE officials say they remain wary of Iranian influence in Iraq. Iranian suspicions of the GCC states could be one explanation why UAE and other GCC airforces are not participating in any airstrikes against the Islamic States in Iraq.

Earlier, the UAE undertook several initiatives to support U.S. efforts to stabilize Iraq after the fall of Saddam Hussein. During 2003-2011, when international forces were helping secure Iraq, the UAE provided facilities for Germany to train Iraqi police. Agreeing with the U.S. view that Sunni Arab states need to engage the Shiite-dominated government in Baghdad, in June 2008, the UAE appointed an Ambassador to Iraq, Abdullah Ibrahim al-Shehi, the first Arab country to do so. Shaykh Mohammad bin Zayid visited Iraq in October 2008. In February 2012, the UAE opened a consulate in the Kurdish region of Iraq which comprises three northern provinces and is administered by the Kurdistan Regional Government (KRG), a legally constituted region within Iraq. During 2003-11, the UAE provided about $215 million for Iraq reconstruction in the form of humanitarian contributions. Some of the funds were used to rebuild hospitals and provide medical treatment to Iraqi children in the UAE. Bilateral trade was estimated at about $5 billion, and UAE companies invested in housing and other projects in Iraq. In July 2008, the UAE wrote off $7 billion (including interest) in Iraqi debt.

Afghanistan and Pakistan

The UAE assists the U.S. and international mission to stabilize Afghanistan with a 250-person contingent of UAE troops serving in Afghanistan since 2003. The UAE forces, the only Arab combat forces in Afghanistan, operate in the restive southern part of Afghanistan, particularly Uruzgan Province, where they have been welcomed by the population. UAE representatives say that UAE forces will remain in Afghanistan alongside any U.S. forces that remain after the end of the current international security mission in 2014. The UAE has a counterpart to the Obama Administration's Special Representative for Afghanistan and Pakistan (SRAP).

The UAE has provided about $350 million in economic aid for Afghanistan since the fall of the Taliban. The projects funded with UAE aid include "Zayed University," a college serving over 6,000 Afghan students per year; six medical clinics; a major hospital with a capacity of 7,000 patients; the building of "Zayed City" that houses 200 Afghan families displaced by violence; 160 drinking wells; and 38 mosques.[31]

Before the September 11, 2001 attacks on the United States, the UAE apparently did not perceive the Taliban movement that was in power there as a major threat. The UAE was one of only three countries (Pakistan and Saudi Arabia were the others) that recognized the Taliban during 1996-2001 as the government of Afghanistan, even though the Taliban regime was harboring Al Qaeda leaders. During Taliban rule, the UAE allowed Ariana Afghan airlines to operate direct service between the two countries. After the September 11, 2001, attacks, the UAE helped the United States oust the Taliban regime from Afghanistan by making available its military facilities for U.S. and allied use, as discussed.

---

[31] Information provided to CRS by the UAE Embassy in Washington, DC, December 2009.

In related aid for U.S. regional policy, the UAE has provided over $800 million to Pakistan since 2001. Abu Dhabi hosted the November 2008 meeting of the "Friends of Pakistan" donors group that jointly helped Pakistan through its financial difficulties. As part of its assistance to Pakistan, the UAE provided about $100 million to aid victims of a major earthquake in Pakistan in October 2005, and about $20 million in 2011 to help victims of flooding there.

Other Regional Issues

The UAE differs with some of its GCC allies, particularly Qatar, on some regional issues, while others regional issues attract broad agreement. To exercise leverage and influence in Arab countries undergoing transition, the UAE has used primarily—although not exclusively—its financial wherewithal.

Bahrain

Within the GCC—a core UAE concern—the UAE has joined other GCC states in supporting the Al Khalifa regime in Bahrain against a Shiite-led uprising. The UAE sent 500 UAE police to join a 1,000 troop Saudi force that deployed to Bahrain in March 2011. At least some of the UAE force remained after that time, because one UAE police officer was killed, along with two Bahrain police, in a Bahrain opposition bombing on March 4, 2014. The UAE, Saudi Arabia, Kuwait, and Qatar also have provided financial help to Bahrain and Oman; Oman faced significant protests in 2011. The G-8 countries have set up a "Transition Fund" to help Bahrain, Oman, and other Arab countries experiencing unrest, and the UAE pledged $5 million to the fund in May 2013.

Egypt

The UAE has aligned with Saudi Arabia in supporting a post-Mubarak political structure in Egypt that is hostile to the Muslim Brotherhood. The UAE strongly opposed the election of a leader of the Muslim Brotherhood, Mohammad Morsi, as President and supported the Egyptian military's ouster of Morsi in July 2013. Within a week of Morsi's ouster, the UAE backed a Saudi effort to financially stabilize the military-led government in Cairo. The UAE pledged $3 billion in assistance as part of the broader Saudi-led package totaling $12 billion ($5 billion from Saudi Arabia and $4 billion from Kuwait, in addition to the UAE funds).

The Egypt issue has been part of a significant rift inside the GCC. Qatar opposed the military-led ouster of Morsi and has criticized the Egyptian military's subsequent crackdown on the Muslim Brotherhood. The differences caused the UAE, Saudi Arabia, and Bahrain to recall their ambassadors from Qatar in March 2014. They returned the ambassadors following an April 2014 agreement that the GCC countries will strive to better coordinate their foreign policies and not work against each other's stated interests.

Libya

To promote political change that the UAE supports, the UAE worked with the United States and other NATO countries and partners to oust Muammar Qadhafi in 2011. The UAE Air Force sent six (a squadron) of its U.S-made F-16s and six Mirage fighters to participate in the NATO-led no-fly zone enforcement and ground target strike operations in Libya. It reportedly sent some weapons to the Libyan rebels.[32] In May 2011, Abu Dhabi hosted a major meeting of Libyan dissident and in June 2011, the UAE formally recognized the Benghazi-based Transitional National Council (TNC) as the sole representative of the Libyan people and pledged financial support to it. In March 2012, the UAE transferred 58 aging Mirage 2000 combat aircraft to the post-Qadhafi government. The UAE has provided about $13 million in aid to post-Qadhafi Libya through the UAE government and UAE charity organizations.

Since Qadhafi's fall, however, Libya has become an arena for significant differences within the GCC states. The intra-GCC dispute over post-Mubarak Egypt has spilled over into major rifts over post-Qadhafi Libya. As Libya has descended into political chaos, the UAE and Qatar each have supported rival militia factions. The military-led government in Egypt has largely sided with the UAE position. In late August 2014, U.S. officials confirmed that the UAE, jointly with Egypt, secretrly carried out airstrikes in Libya against Islamist militias that reportedly enjoy support from Qatar.[33]

Yemen

In Yemen, the UAE joined a high-profile GCC mediation effort that reached an agreement for President Ali Abdullah Saleh to step down in favor of a political transition. President Saleh was injured in an assassination attempt in June 2011 and recuperated in Saudi Arabia, but he returned to the country in November 2011. He later signed the transition agreement and left office on January 22, 2012. However, the UAE and other GCC states express concern about a rebellion led by the Shiite "Houthi" faction that took over large parts of the capital, Sanaa, in September 2014. U.S. officials have asserted that Iran has backed the Houthis and the GCC states see Houthi gains as an opportunity for Iran to exert additional influence on the Arabian Peninsula.

Arab-Israeli Dispute

On the Arab-Israeli issue, the UAE asserts that any settlement between Israel and the Palestinians must be "just" (sufficiently beneficial to the Palestinians). It has sometimes privately criticized the United States as excessively supportive of Israel. UAE leaders publicly backed the Palestinian Authority's bid for statehood recognition at the United Nations General Assembly in September 2011—a proposal the United States opposed as premature and preemptive of Israeli-Palestinian negotiations. In December 2008 and January 2009, the UAE government permitted street demonstrations in support of Hamas during its war with Israel. It also aggressively investigated and, based on evidence developed, formally accused Israel in the killing of a Hamas leader in Dubai in January 2010. However, reflecting the broader intra-GCC schism on regional political Islamist movements, the UAE criticized Qatar's apparent support for Hamas in the July 2014 combat between Hamas in the Gaza Strip and Israel as stoking regional conflict. The UAE cites Qatar's support for Hamas as another example of Qatar's support for Muslim Brotherhood-linked organizations that the UAE asserts are a threat to the GCC states themselves.

The UAE has not advanced its own far-reaching proposals to resolve the Israeli-Palestinian dispute, as has King Abdullah of Saudi Arabia. Nor has UAE tried to directly mediate between

---

[32] James Risen, Mark Mazzetti, and Michael Schmidt. "Militant Forces Got Arms Meant for Libya Rebels." *New York Times*, December 6, 2012.

[33] "U.S. Officials: Egypt, UAE Behind Airstrikes in Libya." Associated Press, August 26, 2014.

Palestinian factions, as have Saudi Arabia, Qatar, or Egypt. In 1994 the UAE joined with the other Gulf monarchies in ending enforcement of the Arab League's boycott of companies doing business with Israel and on companies that deal with companies that do business with Israel. The UAE formally bans direct trade with Israel, although UAE companies reportedly do business with Israeli firms and some Israeli diplomats have attended multilateral meetings in the UAE. Unlike Qatar and Oman, the UAE did not host multilateral Arab-Israeli working groups on regional issues when those talks took place during 1994-1998. In 2007, the UAE joined a "quartet" of Arab states (the others are Saudi Arabia, Egypt, and Jordan) to assist U.S. diplomacy on Israeli-Palestinian issues, and it attended the Annapolis summit on the issue that year. On January 19, 2014, the UAE hosted a conference of the International Renewable Energy Agency (IRENA), attended by Israel's Minister of National Infrastructure, Energy, and Water Silvan Shalom. Iranian delegates attended as well.

The UAE has been a donor to the Palestinians. According to the UAE government, the UAE has provided nearly $550 million to humanitarian projects for Palestinian refugees in the Palestinian territories, and in Syria; the funds have been channeled in part through the U.N. Relief Works Agency (UNRWA). One major UAE action has been to fund a housing project in Rafah, in the Gaza Strip, called "Shaykh Khalifa City."

Other UAE Foreign Aid[34]

The UAE asserts that it has provided billions of dollars in international aid through its government and through funds controlled by royal family members and other elites, aside from funds provided for the specific crises discussed above. Among initiatives outside the Near East and South Asia region:

- In 2012, the UAE, through the government and UAE-based relief groups, spent $1.5 billion in foreign aid worldwide, of which $600 million went to mainly Jordan, the Palestinian territories, Yemen, and Azerbaijan. One fund, the Abu Dhabi Fund for Development (ADFD), established in 1971, has distributed about $3.5 billion to 207 projects in 53 countries. Of this amount, about $240 million was distributed in 2010.

- The UAE provided $100 million to aid victims of the December 2004 tsunami in the Indian Ocean.

- In May 2011, the UAE donated $30 million to the Australian state of Queensland to fund cyclone shelters.

- In July 2011, UAE foundations responded to a U.N. appeal for aid to the victims of a drought in East Africa.

- In February 2012, the UAE announced an additional $2 million donation to the Local Stability Fund that provides relief to victims of conflict in Somalia. In October 2013, the UAE cabinet decided to reopen a UAE embassy in Mogadishu, in part to facilitate the delivery of relief to Somalis.

- The UAE has donated substantial sums for humanitarian causes in the United States, including $150 million for a cancer center at the University of Texas;

---

[34] Factsheet provided by UAE Embassy in Washington, DC, June 2011.

$100 million to assist New Orleans after Hurricane Katrina in 2005; $150 million to a children's medical center in Washington, DC, in 2009; and $1 million worth of Apple laptop computers to the Joplin, Missouri, public schools systems in the wake of the May 2011 tornado there.

Cooperation Against Terrorism and Proliferation

The UAE cooperates extensively with U.S. efforts against a broad range of terrorist activities and proliferation in the region—well beyond cooperation against the Islamic State organization. The United States has sought to help the UAE redress a past pattern of lax enforcement of export and border controls that enabled technology to reach Iran and terrorists to transit and make use of the UAE financial system. The relatively small sums of U.S. aid to UAE that have been provided in recent years have been generally for programs to improve UAE enforcement of export control laws and combat terrorism. No U.S. aid to UAE for these programs was requested for FY2014 or FY2015.

Terrorism Issues

During the mid-1990s, some Al Qaeda activists reportedly were able to move through the UAE.[35] Two of the September 11, 2001, attack hijackers were UAE nationals, and they reportedly used UAE-based financial networks in the plot.

Since the September 11 attacks on the United States, the UAE has been credited in State Department "Country Reports on Terrorism," including the latest one for 2013 (April 30, 2014),[36] with significant efforts against terrorism and terrorism financing. The State Department reports say the UAE has arrested senior Al Qaeda operatives; denounced terror attacks; improved border security; instituted programs to counter violent extremism; investigated suspect financial transactions; criminalized use of the Internet by terrorist groups; and strengthened its bureaucracy and legal framework to combat terrorism. In July 2014, the FNC approved a draft counter-terrorism law that makes it easier to prosecute, and increases penalties for, planning acts of terrorism, and authorizes the UAE cabinet to set up lists of designated terrorist organizations and persons.[37] The draft law was signed into law by President Khalifa on August 21, 2014.

Among notable successes, in early 2009, UAE security officials reportedly broke up an Al Qaeda plot to blow up targets in Dubai emirate.[38] On October 29, 2010, UAE authorities assisted in foiling an Al Qaeda in the Arabian Peninsula plot to send bombs to the United States. On December 26, 2012, the UAE stated that it had arrested members of an alleged terrorist cell plotting attacks in the United States, in an operation conducted in cooperation with Saudi Arabia. In April 2013, UAE authorities arrested seven non-UAE Arab nationals allegedly affiliated with Al Qaeda. In May 2014, the UAE tried nine people on charges of supporting the Al Nusrah Front,

---

[35] Department of State. Office of the Coordinator for Counterterrorism. Country Reports on Terrorism 2013. April 30, 2043. Author conversations with executive branch officials, 1997-2013.

[36] "U.S. Embassy to Reopen on Saturday After UAE Threat." *Reuters*, March 26, 2004.

[37] "UAE Stiffens Counterterror Laws. Defense News, July 26, 2014.

[38] Lake, Eli and Sarah Carter. "UAE Kept Tight Lid on Disrupted Terror Plot." *Washington Times*, September 17, 2009.

a hardline Islamist faction of Syrian rebels with alleged ties to Al Qaeda and which is named by the United States as a Foreign Terrorist Organization (FTO).

The UAE Central Bank's Financial Intelligence Unit is credited in recent State Department terrorism reports with providing training programs to UAE financial institutions on money laundering and terrorism financing, and making mandatory the registration of informal financial transmittal networks (*hawalas*). A law to strengthen the UAE's anti-money laundering efforts is reportedly in the final stages of consideration, and in June 2014 the UAE set up a financial task force to better prevent use of UAE financial institutions by terrorist organizations. In September 2012, the FBI Legal Attache established a sub-office at the U.S. consulate in Dubai to assist with joint efforts against terrorism and terrorism financing.

On December 13-14, 2012, during a meeting of the Global Counterterrorism Forum (GCTF), the UAE-based "International Center of Excellence for Countering Violent Extremism," known as *Hedayah*, was inaugurated. The center is an institution for training, dialogue, collaboration, and research to counter violent extremism. The UAE is a founding member of the GCTF, which was formed in September 2011.

Port and Border Controls

The UAE has signed on to several U.S. efforts to prevent proliferation and terrorism. These include the Container Security Initiative Statement of Principles, aimed at screening U.S.-bound containerized cargo transiting Dubai ports. Under it, three U.S. Customs and Border Protection officers are co-located with the Dubai Customs Intelligence Unit at Port Rashid in Dubai. The program results in about 25 inspections per week of U.S.-bound containers, many of them apparently originating in Iran. The UAE is a party to the Proliferation Security Initiative, the Megaports Initiative designed to prevent terrorist from using major ports to ship illicit material, and the Customs-Trade Partnership Against Terrorism. In 2013, the United States and UAE signed an agreement to establish a "pre-clearance facility" at the Abu Dhabi International Airport for travelers boarding direct flights to the United States.

Export Controls

The UAE record on preventing the reexport of advanced technology, particularly to Iran, has been mixed in past years, but has improved considerably since mid-2010. Taking advantage of geographic proximity and the high volume of Iran-Dubai trade ($10 billion per year), numerous Iranian entities involved in Iran's energy sector and its WMD programs have offices in the UAE that are used to try to procure needed technology and equipment. In connection with revelations of illicit sales of nuclear technology to Iran, Libya, and North Korea by Pakistan's nuclear scientist A.Q. Khan, Dubai was named as a key transfer point for Khan's shipments of nuclear components. Two Dubai-based companies were apparently involved in transshipping components: SMB Computers and Gulf Technical Industries.[39] On April 7, 2004, the Administration sanctioned a UAE firm, Elmstone Service and Trading FZE, for allegedly selling weapons of mass destruction-related technology to Iran, under the Iran-Syria Non-Proliferation Act (P.L. 106-178). In June 2006, the Bureau of Industry and Security (BIS) imposing a license requirement on U.S. exports to Mayrow General Trading Company and related enterprises in the

---

[39] Milhollin, Gary and Kelly Motz. "Nukes 'R' US." *New York Times* op. ed. March 4, 2004.

UAE after Mayrow allegedly transshipped devices used to construct improvised explosive devices (IED) in Iraq and Afghanistan.[40]

In January 2009, the Institute for Science and International Security issued a report entitled "Iranian Entities' Illicit Military Procurement Networks," published January 12, 2009. The report asserted that Iran has used UAE companies to obtain technology from U.S. suppliers, and that the components obtained have been used to construct improvised explosive devices (IEDs) shipped by Iran to militants in Iraq and Afghanistan. Other UAE companies the report alleges were involved in this network included not only Mayrow but also Majidco Micro Electronics, Micatic General Trading, and Talinx Electronics.

The UAE has responded when U.S. officials have threatened to sanction the UAE for lax export control enforcement. In February 2007 the Administration threatened to create a new category of countries called "Destinations of Diversion Control"—countries for which there is determined to be reexportation of controlled technology to Iran and other countries forbidden from receiving such U.S. goods. The UAE was one intended designee country. A June 2010 Iran sanctions law, the Comprehensive Iran Sanctions, Accountability, and Divestment Act (CISADA, P.L. 111-195) set up that category and mandates sanctions on countries determined to be Destinations of Diversion Control.

The improved performance of the UAE on this issue has caused these provisions not to be implemented with respect to the UAE. In September 2007, the FNC adopted a law strengthening export controls, and UAE authorities immediately used that law to shut down 40 foreign and UAE firms allegedly involved in dual use exports to Iran and other countries. On July 22, 2010, Deputy Assistant Secretary of State for International Security and Nonproliferation Vann Van Diepen testified before the House Foreign Affairs Committee's Subcommittee on Terrorism, Nonproliferation and Trade that the UAE had augmented the staff of the office that implements the 2007 law. He added that the UAE's enforcement bodies—customs, law enforcement, and intelligence services—are functioning to that end.[41] In September 2012 the UAE (and Bahrain) impounded shipments to Iran of items that Iran purportedly sought for use in its nuclear program. As a GCC member, the UAE participates in the U.S.-GCC Counterproliferation Workshop.

The issue of leakage of technology has sometimes caused U.S. criticism or questioning of UAE investment deals. In December 2008, some Members of Congress called for a review by the inter-agency Committee on Foreign Investment in the United States (CFIUS) of a proposed joint venture between Advanced Micro Devices and Advanced Technology Investment Co. of Abu Dhabi for the potential for technology transfers. In February 2006, CFIUS approved the takeover by the Dubai-owned "Dubai Ports World" company of a British firm that manages six U.S. port facilities. Members of Congress, concerned that the takeover might weaken U.S. port security, opposed it in P.L. 109-234, causing the company to divest assets involved in U.S. port operations (divestment completed in late 2006 to AIG Global Investments). Little opposition was expressed to a November 2007 investment of $7.5 billion by the Abu Dhabi Investment Authority (ADIA) in Citigroup, which was then troubled by the global financial crisis.

---

[40] BIS, "General Order Concerning Mayrow General Trading and Related Enterprises," 71 *Federal Register* 107, June 5, 2006.

[41] Testimony of Mr. Vann Van Diepen before the House Foreign Affairs Committee. July 22, 2010.

Nuclear Agreement and other Technology Issues[42]

The government of the United Arab Emirates (UAE) announced in 2008 that it would acquire its first nuclear power reactors to satisfy projected increases in domestic electricity demand.[43] The United States and the UAE signed an agreement on January 15, 2009, to help the UAE develop a nuclear power program. Some in Congress expressed concerns about this agreement because of fears of potential leakage of technology to Iran as well as the potential for additional regional proliferation of nuclear technology.

Policy makers and advisers in the government of Abu Dhabi, in consultation with representatives from the other six emirates, are guiding the program's implementation to achieve what experts call a "gold standard" a nuclear project with no proliferation potential. A number of U.S. and European firms have secured administrative and financial advisory contracts with the program. The agreement for the United States to assist the program, subject to conditions specified in Section 123 of the Atomic Energy Act of 1954 [42 U.S.C. 2153(b)], was signed by the Obama Administration on May 21, 2009 (and submitted to Congress that day). Several congressional resolutions approving the agreement (S.J.Res. 18 and H.J.Res. 60) were introduced, compared to only one disapproving (H.J.Res. 55). No measure blocking the agreement was enacted within 90 days of the submission of the agreement to Congress, and the "1-2-3 Agreement" entered into force on December 17, 2009.

In January 2010, the UAE announced that it had chosen the Korea Electric Power Corporation (KEPCO of South Korea) to construct the first of four APR1400 nuclear reactors that would sell electricity to the Abu Dhabi Water and Electricity Authority. The first plant is expected to start operating in 2017 and the other three are scheduled to be completed and operational by 2020, according to the UAE.[44] The plant construction is taking place near Abu Dhabi's western border with Saudi Arabia.[45]

The Emirates Nuclear Energy Corporation (ENEC) announced in July 2011 that it has begun a "procurement competition" to obtain fuel supplies for the four proposed reactors.[46] "The final contracts are expected to be signed in the first quarter of 2012," according to the ENEC. No specific decisions have been made regarding the disposition of spent reactor fuel. The UAE has committed to refrain from domestic uranium enrichment and reprocessing spent nuclear reactor fuel. Enrichment and reprocessing are considered to the most sensitive parts of the nuclear fuel cycle because they can both produce fissile material for nuclear weapons.

The International Atomic Energy Agency announced December 14, 2011, that a group of experts had completed a review of the UAE's "regulatory framework for nuclear safety and radiation

---

[42] This section was prepared by Paul Kerr, Analyst in Weapons of Mass Destruction Nonproliferation, CRS. See CRS Report R40344, *The United Arab Emirates Nuclear Program and Proposed U.S. Nuclear Cooperation*, by Christopher M. Blanchard and Paul K. Kerr.

[43] UAE officials estimate that their country must expand its power generation and transmission capacity from the current level of 16 gigawatts to 40 gigawatts by 2020 in order to meet projected demand increases

[44] http://enec.gov.ae/our-nuclear-energy-program/prime-contractor/.

[45] http://enec.gov.ae/our-nuclear-energy-program/preferred-site/.

[46] http://www.enec.gov.ae/media-centre/news/content/emirates-nuclear-energy-corporation-begins-nuclear-fuel-procurement-co.

protection." Providing further reassurances to U.S. officials, the review both "noted good practices" and provided suggestions to the Federal Authority for Nuclear Regulation, the UAE's nuclear regulatory authority.[47]

On other technology issues, in July 2014 the UAE announced it will form a "UAE Space Agency." The agency is to enjoy full financial and administrative independence.[48] According to the government, by 2021 the agency is to launch an unmanned spaceship from the Arabian peninsula that will probe Mars.

Economic Issues

The UAE, a member of the World Trade Organization (WTO), has developed a free market economy, but one that is widely considered weakly regulated. Partly as a result, the UAE, particularly Dubai emirate, pursued economic strategies built on attracting investment to construct large numbers of opulent and futuristic projects designed to attract expatriates and international tourists. The UAE is participating in Gulf-wide economic infrastructure projects such as a railroad network connecting all the GCC states, to become operational by 2017.

The UAE economy was affected significantly by the 2007-2009 global financial crisis, which caused widespread layoffs in UAE and the departure of thousands of foreign workers, and left UAE banks with vast amounts of nonperforming loans.[49] The downturn in real estate prices also affected regional investors, such as those in Afghanistan, who bought into high-end housing such as on the Palm Islands. The fall in value nearly caused a collapse of a major Afghan bank, Kabul Bank, in September 2010.

To address the crisis, the federal government took on some public debt and drew upon some of the country's purported $700 billion invested in "sovereign wealth funds" to inject into Dubai banks to help them ride out the downturn. The largest such fund, called Mubadala, is owned and run by Abu Dhabi. However, by the end of 2011, the UAE's worst economic problems were behind it and its growth improved substantially to about 3.3% for all of 2011. Growth was about 4% for 2013, according to the IMF.

Oil and Gas Sector and "Clean Energy" Initiatives

The source of the UAE's sovereign wealth has been oil sales. Abu Dhabi has 80% of the federation's proven oil reserves of about 100 billion barrels, enough for over 100 years of exports at the current production rate of about 2.5 million–2.7 million barrels per day (mbd). Of that, over 2 mbd are exported, and the UAE may have as much as 500,000 bpd of spare capacity.[50] The United States imported no UAE crude oil in 2012 or 2013, and only a small amount in 2011 (about 2.4 million barrels for the entire year). The largest share of UAE oil goes to Japan. The UAE has vast quantities of natural gas but consumes more than it produces. It has entered into a

---

[47] http://www.iaea.org/press/?p=2572.

[48] "UAE Wants Space Agency and Probe to Mars by 2021." *Russia Today*, July 16, 2014.

[49] Worth, Robert. "Laid Off Foreigners Flee as Dubai Spirals Down." *New York Times*, February 12, 2008.

[50] http://www.thenational.ae/events/areas/abu-dhabi/adnoc-preserves-spare-supplies.

deal (Dolphin project) with neighboring countries under which a recently constructed pipeline carries natural gas from the large gas exporter, Qatar, to the UAE and on to Oman as well.

In addition, the UAE is trying to secure its oil export routes against any threat by Iran to close the strategic Strait of Hormuz, through with the UAE and other major oil exporters transport their oil exports. In mid-July 2012, the UAE loaded its first tanker of oil following completion of the Abu Dhabi Crude Oil Pipeline (ADCOP) which terminates in the emirate of Fujairah, on the Gulf of Oman. The line, which cost $3 billion, has a capacity to transport 1.5 million barrels per day of crude oil—about half of the UAE's peak production. The UAE is also planning a large refinery near that terminal, and possibly a second oil pipeline exiting there, to further secure its oil exports and value-added petroleum products.[51]

Seeking to reinvest its oil wealth, Abu Dhabi has sought in recent years to outdo Dubai by building local branches of famous U.S. and European museums. However, it has also tried to use its oil wealth to plan for a time when the developed world is no longer reliant on oil imports. It has funded "Masdar City"—a project, the first phase of which is to be completed in 2015, to build a planned city which will rely only on renewable energy sources. Automobiles that run on fossil fuels are banned from Masdar City. One feature of the city is a system of driverless taxis that use automation to take passengers to their destinations.

U.S.-UAE Trade and Trade Promotion Discussions

U.S. trade with the UAE is a significant issue because the UAE is the largest market for U.S. exports to the Middle East. In 2013, U.S. firms exported about $24.6 billion worth of goods to the UAE. Over 1,000 U.S. companies have offices there and there are 60,000 Americans working in UAE. U.S. exports to UAE in coming years (2014-2018) are expected to be very large because of a spate of orders for U.S. commercial aircraft in 2013 by expanding UAE airlines Emirates Air and Ettihad Airlines. Many of these orders were placed at the Dubai Air Show in November 2013.

On November 15, 2004, the Administration notified Congress it had begun negotiating a free trade agreement (FTA) with the UAE. Several rounds of talks were held prior to the June 2007 expiration of Administration "trade promotion authority," but progress was halting. The FTA talks have been replaced by a U.S.-UAE "Economic Policy Dialogue," involving the major U.S. economic departments and their UAE counterparts. The dialogue, consisting of two meetings per year, began in late 2011 and also included discussion of reform of UAE export controls, an issue discussed above. In addition, as part of the GCC, the UAE is negotiating with the United States a "GCC-U.S. Framework Agreement on Trade, Economic, Investment, and Technical Cooperation," an umbrella instrument for promoting ties between the two sides in the economic area—essentially a GCC-wide trade and investment framework agreement (TIFA). The negotiations were led by the U.S. Trade Representative (USTR), and an agreement was signed on September 25, 2012.

The UAE, which is considered wealthy, has received small amounts of U.S. assistance. The primary purpose of the aid is to make the UAE eligible for advice and programming to improve its border security and export controls, as shown below. None has been requested since FY2011.

---

[51] "Abu Dhabi: In the Pipeline." The Middle East, January 26, 2012.

Table 2. Recent U.S. Aid to UAE

(in thousands of dollars)

	FY07	FY08	FY09	FY10	FY11	FY12	FY13	FY14	FY15 (req)
NADR (Nonproliferation, Anti-Terrorism, Demining, and Related)— Counterterrorism Programs (ATA)	1,409		725						
NADR- Combating WMD	172	300	200	230	230				
International Military Education and Training (IMET)				10					
Totals	**1,581**	**300**	**925**	**240**	**230**	**0**	**0**	**0**	**0**

Author Contact Information

Kenneth Katzman
Specialist in Middle Eastern Affairs
kkatzman@crs.loc.gov, 7-7612